Country House Life

A CENTURY IN PHOTOGRAPHS

Country House Life

A CENTURY IN PHOTOGRAPHS

Elizabeth Drury
and Francesca Scoones

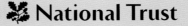
National Trust

First published in the United Kingdom in 2012 by
National Trust Books
10 Southcombe Street
London W14 0RA

An imprint of Anova Books Ltd

ISBN: 9781907892257

A CIP catalogue record for this book is
available from the British Library.

20 19 18 17 16 15 14 13 12
10 9 8 7 6 5 4 3 2 1

Colour reproduction by Mission Productions, Hong Kong
Printed by Toppan Leefung, China

This book can be ordered direct from the publisher at the website:
www.anovabooks.com, or try your local bookshop. Also available
at National Trust shops, including www.nationaltrustbooks.co.uk.

Right: King Fuad of Egypt at Polesden Lacey, where he
stayed from 27th–29th July 1929 as the guest of Mrs
Ronnie Greville. Mrs Greville had visited Egypt and met
members of the royal family.

Previous page: Lady Victoria, Lady Albertha and Lady Edith
Edgcumbe, daughters of the 4th Earl of Mount Edgcumbe,
photographed with a pet springbok in c. 1875. The Mount
Edgcumbes owned Cotehele, which came to the National Trust in
1947, and Mount Edgcumbe, both in Cornwall.

Contents

Introduction

A photograph taken long ago is a precious thing; it is a moment in time made visible, a record of a person, occasion or place that someone wanted to remember. It evokes the past in a way that is more immediate and more powerful than words.

The photographs in this book, taken between the 1840s and 1940s, are of people who lived and worked in the country houses which now belong to the National Trust, and of their friends, neighbours and guests. They provide a glimpse of not just where but how those people lived: the Egertons at Tatton Park in Cheshire, the Agar-Robartes at Lanhydrock in Cornwall, the Angleseys at Plas Newydd on Anglesey, and many others.

The families employed large numbers of people as household servants and as gardeners, gatekeepers, gamekeepers and foresters. In autumn and winter they amused themselves hunting and shooting and in the summer picnicking and playing cricket, tennis and croquet. They travelled by steam train and horse-drawn carriage and later in motor cars; they entertained on a grand scale; they organised amateur theatricals. Their children were looked after by nurses and taught by tutors and governesses.

Over time, restrictive and elaborate clothing such as crinolines and stovepipe hats was replaced by dresses, suits and hats appropriate for activity rather than purely for following the prevailing fashion. Female indoor servants started to wear aprons and caps more suitable for their work than the cast-off clothes of their mistress, and the braid, epaulettes and powdered hair of the footmen gave way to simpler attire.

The earliest photograph reproduced in the book, a calotype, was taken by William Henry Fox Talbot at his home, Lacock Abbey in Wiltshire. It dates from the pioneering years of photography when almost every picture was a scientific experiment – though artistry was involved in positioning the subjects, who were obliged to remain utterly immobile for up to ten minutes for a single exposure. As a result, they tend to look almost like statues rather than animate human beings.

Early cameras were large, heavy, wooden boxes mounted on stands. From the 1850s the accessories required to produce a print included the glass plates that were replacing Fox Talbot's paper negatives, collodion solution to make the plates light-sensitive and further chemicals to develop the prints. Formal portraits and *cartes-de-visite* were taken in a studio by

A group outside Lacock Abbey in Wiltshire, a calotype made by William Henry Fox Talbot in the 1840s. With the calotype process, which he invented, more than one print could be made from the same negative.

Right: Rosalie Chichester with her camera at Arlington Court, Devon, in the late nineteenth century. She took photographs of people and events on the estate, plants and animals, pasting many of them into albums.

H.M.Ward. M.Ward. Bertha Jane Ward.

Above: Mary Ward with two of her children at Castle Ward, Co.Down, in 1861. She took the photograph herself with a delayed exposure, hence the impression that she had grabbed the child looking away from the camera at the last moment.

professional photographers, who would also be summoned to a country house to photograph the family at the time of a christening or other special event, or to record the visit of notable personages such as a member of the royal family.

Some of the earliest amateur photographers were women with time to spare, enquiring minds and an interest in science. Mary Ward, daughter-in-law of the 3rd Viscount Bangor of Castle Ward in Northern Ireland, was a painter, naturalist, astronomer, pioneer of the microscope and published writer and illustrator, as well as a photographer. Underneath a print of herself with two of her children she wrote, 'Photographed by M J Ward April 1st 1861, on which day the chemicals were for some reason in a highly sensitive state as negatives as above were taken in 2 seconds.'

Rosalie Chichester led a solitary life as an only child and, later, as the unmarried owner of Arlington Court in Devon. She collected fossils and shells, and taught herself to take and develop photographs. Born in 1865, she lived until 1949, half a century after the invention of small portable cameras. The Kodak camera using roll film had been invented in America by George Eastman in 1888. By the early twentieth century his company's easy-to-use Box Brownie had arrived in Britain and

it was suddenly possible for anyone who could afford to buy one to take photographs on the spur of the moment.

From this period there is a naturalness about the people in the photographs. In these spontaneous images it is easier to tell what the subjects were really like, not just what they looked like in their finest clothes, as shown in the stiff portraits of the 1870s and 1880s. There is humour, and emotion, too, in the exhilaration of a group of cyclists and of a Land Girl during The Second World War, one of the latest photographs in the book.

Country house photographs survive in albums and visitors' books, along with once-treasured portraits that were sometimes removed from their frames and stored in boxes. In addition to these sources, former members of staff who were employed in country houses and their descendants have been generous in donating photographs to the National Trust in recent years. Together, these images illustrate a way of life that is now history.

Almost all the houses where the pictures were taken survive; it is the men, women and children who lived and worked in them long ago who are missing. They are rediscovered in the photographs chosen for this book.

The Families

In the mid-nineteenth century the owner of a country house and estate still held a position of social standing and, if he chose to exercise it, political influence. He might have a seat in the House of Commons as an elected Member of Parliament or the hereditary right to sit in the House of Lords as a peer; he might serve as a magistrate or colonel of the militia and take on other local public duties. As lord of the manor he could own one or more church livings, which carried the right to appoint the incumbent; country parsons were often younger sons of the nobility and gentry. He gave employment to many people and the land was farmed by his tenants.

Engagement in political affairs was a tradition in the Trevelyan family of Wallington in Northumberland. Charles Edward Trevelyan reformed the Civil Service, served as an administrator in India, and was rewarded with a baronetcy. His son, Sir George Otto, and grandson, another Sir Charles, were Liberal Members of Parliament. For over 100 years the Aclands from Killerton in Devon also served as Liberal Members of Parliament and Sir Richard Acland, the 15th Baronet, tried to sell his estates to fund a radical party of his own. Increasingly, though, the old county families served their communities on the local rather than the national stage. Their interests might embrace art, literature, science, horticulture or agriculture, and almost always included sport.

The Regency age of extravagance had placed a great strain on the resources of many families. A visitor to Attingham in Shropshire in the 1860s recorded the deserted stable yard overrun with rats and a single light burning in the house. In 1863 John Ketton, who had made a fortune from oil cake, bought the encumbered Felbrigg estate in Norfolk from 'Mad' Windham, whose support of racing and an ill-considered marriage with an adventuress had dissipated what survived of the family's fortune. 'Windham is gone to the dogs, Felbrigg is gone to the Kittens,' quipped a Norfolk neighbour, the Rev. B. J. Armstrong.

For families solely dependent on agricultural land the 1880s proved disastrous. Cheap imports of corn from America so depressed the price of British crops that some families faced ruin and many country houses were sold or rented out. Families who managed to hold on to their estates are chronicled in their declining years on horseback, out shooting or brandishing tennis rackets.

A few families were well buttressed from such financial downturns by the diversity of their financial interests, among them the Hoares of Stourhead, a successful banking family, the Brownlows of Belton, who had inherited Ashridge Park, Hertfordshire, with an income of £70,000 per annum, and the Egertons of Tatton Park, Cheshire, with a large urban rent roll from their land in Stockport.

As the old landed families sold up, their estates were bought and new houses built by men who had prospered in commerce and industry. Some, such as Antony Gibbs of Tyntesfield in Somerset and Sir William Armstrong of Cragside in Northumberland, came from the local gentry. Baron Ferdinand de Rothschild of Waddesdon Manor in Buckinghamshire was a member of a great European banking dynasty, while the fortune that enabled Charles Paget Wade to buy Snowshill in Gloucestershire came from the West Indian sugar plantations he had inherited.

Passing on the great houses to the next generation required not only the money to support the house, but also an heir. In some cases an entail on an estate determined that only a male could inherit and the estate would then pass to a kinsman, as happened at Belton in Lincolnshire, Ickworth in Suffolk and Wallington in Northumberland, to name but a few. Where a daughter might inherit it was sometimes a condition of the inheritance that she keep the family name or add the family name to that of her husband, hence the frequency of double-barrelled names.

Sometimes, as at Uppark in West Sussex, the inheritance was convoluted. The septuagenarian Sir Harry Fetherstonhaugh married his dairymaid, Mary Anne Bullock, in 1825. After Sir Harry's death Mary Anne shared the house with her younger sister Frances. Frances inherited the estate and chose as her heir a neighbour, the Hon. Keith Turnour, younger son of Earl Winterton. A condition of his inheritance was that he add Fetherstonhaugh to his name. The First World War cut a great swathe through the young men of England and many a family lost the heir, including the Hoares of Stourhead in Wiltshire and the Drewes of Castle Drogo in Devon.

Introducing an American bride into the family might bring to a house new standards of comfort: bathrooms, sometimes *en-suite* with the bedrooms, and central heating, and a style of decoration often created by the new breed of interior decorators. Cliveden in Buckinghamshire and Plas Newydd on Anglesey in the years between the wars became bywords for luxurious country house living.

Victoria Sackville-West seated at the centre of a family group at Knole in Kent, *c.* 1900.
Behind her stands her father Lionel, 2nd Lord Sackville. He had welcomed the marriage
between Victoria, his illegitimate daughter, and his nephew and heir Lionel, standing at the
far right. Their daughter Vita is sitting on the arm of her mother's chair.

Lady Adelaide Chetwynd-Talbot and Earl Brownlow at Ashridge Park at the time of their engagement in 1868. They would live at Ashridge in Hertfordshire and at Belton House in Lincolnshire, where they restored the house and laid out the Italian Garden.

William 'Uffy', Earl of Craven, with his favourite bulldog, The Saint, photographed in 1888. The Cravens divided their time between Ashdown House in Oxfordshire and Combe Abbey in Warwickshire.

The Blathwayt family at Dyrham Park, Gloucestershire, *c.* 1880. At the back is Captain George Blathwayt wearing a white hat and at the front on the left his wife Charlotte holding a tennis racquet,

The family at breakfast in the library at Ickworth, Sufolk, December 2nd 1872, 10.30 a.m.
The Marquess and Marchioness of Bristol sit with their backs to the window. The Marquess's
unmarried sister, Lady Mary, is at the head of the table, his brother Lord Augustus and his wife
are seated and facing the window. The gentlemen guests are dressed in tweeds for shooting.

EARL AND COUNTESS OF STAMFORD," LORD GREY OF GROBY AND LADY JANE GREY.   110.

Left: The Earl and Countess of Stamford with their children, Roger, Lord Grey of Groby, and Lady Jane Grey, outside the orangery at Dunham Massey, Cheshire, in 1906. This was the year they moved into the house. The Earl would die in 1910 and be succeeded as the 10th Earl by his son, aged just fourteen.

Sir Henry Dryden, known as 'the Antiquary' for his meticulous study of his ancient house, Canons Ashby in Northamptonshire, with his wife and their daughter Alice, *c.* 1885. He was squire from 1837 until his death in 1899.

Emily Langton Massingberd at Gunby Hall, Lincolnshire, with her three older children, Stephen, Mildred and Mary, in 1878. A keen amateur actress, Emily took the town hall in Bournemouth each year to put on a season of plays with herself in the leading role, often in male attire.

Right: Mrs Chichester and her daughter Rosalie, born in 1865. Rosalie inherited Arlington Court in Devon, at the age of 15, on her father's death in 1881. The estate was heavily in debt and she had to make severe retrenchments.

Above: Sir Vauncey Harpur-Crewe at Calke Abbey. Birds alive, or dead and stuffed – many of them shot by him – were his abiding passion. He was the last of his line and died in 1924.

Mr and Mrs Edward Dering with a manservant in *c.* 1885. Rebecca Orpen had been brought up by her aunt Lady Chatterton. Edward Dering asked for Rebecca's hand but Lady Chatterton chose to accept his proposal herself. Rebecca then married Marmion Ferrers, of an ancient but impoverished Catholic family, in whose moated house, Baddesley Clinton, Warwickshire, the two couples lived until the deaths of their respective spouses allowed Rebecca and Edward to marry.

P. J. Trevelyan
Walter Calverley Trevelyan

Above: Sir Charles Thomas Dyke Acland at Killerton, Devon, with his wife and great-nephews and niece, Richard, Geoffrey, Cuthbert and Eleanor, Christmas 1917. Sir Charles, having no children, was succeeded by his brother and then by Richard.

Left: Sir Walter Calverley Trevelyan and his wife Pauline in c. 1863. He inherited a baronetcy and the two estates of Nettlecombe in Somerset and Wallington in Northumberland in 1846. At Wallington the artistic Pauline painted the piers with native plants while her friend William Bell Scott decorated the roofed-in courtyard with scenes from Northumberland's history. After Sir Walter's death in 1879 Wallington was inherited by a nephew, Charles Edward Trevelyan, created a baronet in his own right.

The Husseys by the steps of the Old Castle at Scotney, Kent, *c.* 1886. Edward Hussey stands on the right with his wife Henrietta to the left of him. Their eldest son, Edward Windsor Hussey, stands on the left. The two dogs are Pepper and Badger.

Left: The eight children of Antony Gibbs with friends, July 1894. Antony succeeded his father at Tyntesfield, Somerset, in 1875. He moved the smoking room from the top of the tower to a new billiard-room with a table by Plucknett of Warwick, centrally heated to ensure faster running of the balls.

Right: Marion and Getrude Ketton in the conservatory at Felbrigg Hall. They were taken to Paris by their aunt to buy the latest fashions.

Below: Marion and Gertrude, the two youngest Ketton daughters at the main south entrance to Felbrigg Hall, Norfolk, soon after their brother Robert inherited the house in 1872. They lived here with him until their untimely deaths in 1895 and 1898 respectively.

The Marquess of Bristol, and his daughter Lady Katherine Hervey in *c.* 1870. He had only daughters and on his death the title and the Ickworth estate passed to his nephew.

Above: Mrs Keith Turnour-Fetherstonhaugh and her daughter Beatrice at Uppark, West Sussex, in *c.* 1905.

Right: Ellen Helyar Phelips with her granddaughter Marjorie Ingilby (*née* Phelips) and baby Cecily at Montacute House, Somerset, in 1905. Ellen Helyar, an heiress, had married William Phelips in 1845. He was a compulsive gambler and sold much of the estate, and by the 1860s he was descending into madness. He died in 1889 and his widow lived on in the house with her grown-up children.

Left: Sir Henry and Lady Hoare with their son Harry and dog Sweep at Stourhead, Wiltshire, in 1912. Harry enlisted in the first days of the First World War. He died in hospital in Alexandria in December 1917 from wounds received at Mughair Ridge the previous month. He was the Hoares' only child.

Lionel with Ben & Nigel Stone Court. 12 Jan 1918

Above: Lionel, 3rd Lord Sackville, with his grandsons Ben and Nigel Nicolson, in the Stone Court at Knole in 1918. Had the boys' mother Vita been a boy she would have inherited Knole.

Lady Berwick on the steps at Attingham Park, Shropshire, in 1921. She was the beautiful daughter of an artist and a half-Italian mother. Her upbringing amongst a circle of artists and writers sojourning in Italy in the late nineteenth century helped to cultivate her taste and inspired the restoration she and her husband carried out at Attingham, the family seat.

Henrietta Jenny Fraser was a famous beauty, known in the fashionable resorts of Ostend and Bad Homburg as 'la belle Anglaise'. Photographed here in full evening dress, she married the much older Walter Ralph Bankes of Kingston Lacy, Dorset, in 1897.

Baron Ferdinand de Rothschild with his dog Poupon. Between 1874 and 1889 Gabriel-Hippolyte Alexandre Destailleur, a French architect, designed Waddesdon Manor in Buckinghamshire, inspired by the châteaux of the Loire. Baron Ferdinand filled it with panelling, furniture, paintings, sculpture, books and objects, largely of the French eighteenth century.

The Houses

The mid-nineteenth century was a period in which great fortunes were made in manufacturing, banking, brewing and trade. Old houses were modernised and new ones were commissioned by men who made their fortunes in cities but aspired to the life and pursuits of a country gentleman.

The arrival of the railway changed social life. Visitors could conveniently come for a short stay and a much wider circle of friends and relations could be assembled. Large numbers of guests with attendant valets, lady's maids and nursemaids required the expansion of the house for both their accommodation and entertainment. Conservatories and billiard-rooms became popular and the halls of grand houses, equipped with large, comfortable sofas, acted as informal gathering places for plays, concerts or dances.

A greater specialisation of the service areas, which were divided between men's and women's work, dictated the layout and size of the domestic wings that were added to some houses. Few, though, boasted the amenities of Cragside in Northumberland, where an electric turn-spit and hydraulic-powered lift were installed.

The Victorian Age heralded a new domesticity. A growing understanding of the most common causes of death meant that more children of wealthy families survived into adulthood. Large families became the norm and children had rooms near to their parents that were fitted out for their comfort and instruction.

After the agricultural depression of the 1880s an estate looked a far less enticing investment, and a house in the country with just enough land to provide a garden and perhaps a day's shooting became the ambition for the modern man. If it was in easy reach of a station with a good service to London he could still go daily to the office or attend Parliament. A grey stone manor house was the ideal retreat, as exemplified in the pages of *Country Life*, first published in 1897. These were sought out and restored by wealthy individuals, some of whom were no doubt keen to give an impression of ancient lineage.

The First World War did not put a stop to country house life, but the style became increasingly informal. Swimming, sunbathing and jazz on the gramophone were the entertainment at houses such as Coleton Fishacre near Totnes, built for the D'Oyly Carte family in 1925.

Scotney Castle, Kent, *c.* 1854, built for Edward Hussey and designed by
Anthony Salvin in the newly fashionable Tudor Revival style. The site was chosen
by William Sawrey Gilpin for the views of the picturesque Old Castle.

Above: The Hon. Catherine Kay-Shuttleworth doing her needlework in the drawing room at Gawthorpe Hall, Lancashire. One of a series of romantic photographs taken by her sister Nina at the time of the visit of King George V and Queen Mary in 1913.

Right: Victoria Sackville-West spinning, one of the photographs taken of her at Knole, Kent, in 1889, the year her father came into his inheritance and she was installed as mistress of the house.

Left: Dunster Castle, during building works, *c.* 1869. George Luttrell inherited Dunster in 1867 and soon afterwards approached Salvin to add a north tower to contain new kitchens in the basement and a nursery wing on the upper floor and romantically crown the rooftop with crenellations.

Graham Baron Ash with his father Alfred Ash and grandfather Joseph Ash in the hall at Packwood House, Warwickshire, shortly after Alfred had bought the house in 1905. Alfred and his son devoted their lives to restoring and furnishing the property.

Sir Geoffrey Mander and his second wife Rosalie with their two children, John and Anthea, in the library at Wightwick Manor, West Midlands, in the 1940s. The house, built by Sir Geoffrey's father Theodore Mander, the paint manufacturer, was much inspired by the Arts and Crafts Movement.

Left: Julius Drewe and Edwin Lutyens surveying the site for Castle Drogo, Devon, in 1910. A defensible high ridge was chosen to the west of the village of Drewsteignton, which was supposedly named after the Norman baron Drogo de Teign, from whom Julius Drewe, with more romance than genealogical accuracy, traced his descent.

Right: Margaret 'Maggie' Beale, daughter of James Beale, the builder of Standen, West Sussex, spinning in the drawing room, c.1910. She was a skilled embroiderer and examples of her work survive in the house, where she lived until her death in 1947.

Far right: Mrs Algernon Sidney Field, mother-in-law of James Beale, sewing in the conservatory at Standen. The house, built in 1892–94, was in easy reach of the station at East Grinstead. James Beale practised as a solicitor in London.

Lady Berwick, on the right, with two friends from Italy, Elbyth
Capponi and Maria Pia Monari, in the Picture Gallery at Attingham
Park, Shropshire, furnished with Caroline Murat's white and gold
Neapolitan furniture purchased by the 3rd Lord Berwick when he
was ambassador in Naples. The photograph was taken in 1924.

Rex Whistler sketching what would later become the mural in the new dining room at Plas Newydd, Anglesey in September 1936. With him is Lady Caroline Paget. The creation of this room was one of the major improvements to the house effected by the 6th Marquess of Anglesey and his wife in the 1930s.

Great Chalfield Manor, Wiltshire, undergoing restoration in 1908. The late fifteenth-century manor house was in a poor state when George Fuller MP purchased the estate in 1878. In 1908 he sold the house to his fourth son Robert, who undertook the restoration and rebuilt the lost east range.

Left: Walford & Spokes, a firm of builders based in Oxford, working on the restoration of Ightham Mote, Kent, in 1890. The manor house had been purchased the previous year from the executors of Charles Selby-Bigge by Thomas Colyer-Fergusson.

Above: Robert and Mabel Fuller at Great Chalfield Manor in 1938. Their meticulous restoration and furnishing of the house is chronicled in James Lees-Milne's diaries.

Charles Paget Wade repairing one of the models from his collection at Snowshill Manor, Gloucestershire, shortly after he had purchased the house in 1919. Wade trained as an architect and devoted his life to forming a vast collection of diverse objects. His range of interests was extraordinary, and so too was his manner of living, devoid of any modern convenience.

Kipling writing in his study at Bateman's in East Sussex in 1935. He bought the Jacobean house in 1902. *Puck of Pook's Hill*, a celebration of Sussex and all that he cherished, was written here.

Vita Sackville-West and Harold Nicolson in the Tower Room at Sissinghurst Castle, Kent. They found the ruin of a splendid Elizabethan house in 1930. Within the ancient walls they created one of the iconic gardens of the twentieth century, and in her writing room in the tower, overlooking the garden, Vita wrote her novels, poetry and influential weekly gardening column.

Left: The Churchill family and friends in the dining room at Chartwell in Kent in *c.* 1928. Churchill's painting *Tea at Chartwell* was based on the photograph. He bought Chartwell in 1922 as a place to retreat to and as a family home.

Above: The D'Oyly Carte family with their dalmatians on the terrace at Coleton Fishacre, *c.* 1930. The house was built at the head of the Dart estuary in Devon by Oswald Milne in 1925–26 for Rupert D'Oyly Carte, son of the impresario, and his wife Lady Dorothy.

Visitors and House Parties

Entertaining was an important aspect of country house life, at its most lavish in the Edwardian era. The extravagance had begun in the last decades of Queen Victoria's reign to keep pace with the tastes of her pleasure-loving eldest son and the Marlborough House Set. A visit from the Prince of Wales, later to become King Edward VII, was widely reported and represented the peak of a hostess's social ambitions; other members of the royal family, foreign heads of state, diplomats, politicians and eminent figures from the world of the arts – in that order – were lesser prizes. Among those who were famous for their house parties were Mrs Ronnie Greville, who lived at Polesden Lacey in Surrey, and Mrs Walter Bankes of Kingston Lacy in Dorset.

The parents of a girl of a marriageable age would arrange for her to meet 'suitable' young men in the informal atmosphere of a house party. The heir to a great estate was much in demand, his every move watched with an eagle eye by his hostess for any indications of a blossoming attachment.

The 'Saturday to Monday' was often built around some particular event: in the autumn it might be a race meeting, in the winter a shoot or a lawn-meet, when the local hunt would gather for a stirrup-cup in front of the house, and in the summer a cricket match. Strolling in the gardens, picnicking, boating on the lake, playing tennis or croquet and attending the village fête or a local show were all summer diversions, requiring as many as three changes of clothing in one day.

In the morning – except on Sundays when attendance at church was mandatory – the men would attempt to prove themselves fine sportsmen while the ladies did their needlework, read, wrote letters or gossiped. Their wardrobes required careful thought and the merits of their dressmakers would be assessed as the ladies entered the drawing room before dinner. Attired in the latest fashion, elaborately coiffed and wearing their husband's family jewellery, they hoped to be greeted with a murmur of admiration. During dinner with its many courses they were expected to enthral their neighbours with their conversation, dazzle with their smiles and engage in mild flirtation.

Also recorded in photographs are the musical and costumed entertainments that were put on during the day or, more often, after dinner. In the 1920s, dressing up to amuse by appearing as ridiculous as possible was a favourite pastime. At a house party guests either participated themselves or were spectators at a performance put on specially for them.

Previous page: The Prince of Wales (later Edward VII) to the left of the table at Waddesdon Manor, Buckinghamshire, in the 1880s. He was the guest of Baron Ferdinand de Rothschild.

Above: Princess May (later Princess of Wales and afterwards Queen Mary) on a visit to Tatton Park, Cheshire, at the invitation of Lord Egerton, a photograph of 1887 from the visitors' book. She stands to the right of her mother, the Duchess of Teck.

Above: The visit of the Princess of Wales to Kingston Lacy, Dorset, in 1908.
She was the guest of Mrs Walter Bankes, sitting second on the left between
her son Ralph and daughter Viola; Daphne stands on the right.

Below: Queen Mary at Packwood House,
Warwickshire, in 1927.

Above: Edward VII with some of his favourite lady friends at
Polesden Lacey, Surrey, in 1909. The Hon. Mrs Ronald Greville,
his hostess, sits on his right; the Hon. Mrs George Keppel, the
King's mistress, is seated second on his left.

Right: The Duke and Duchess of York (later King George VI
and Queen Elizabeth) spent part of their honeymoon in April
1923 at Polesden Lacey, lent to them by Mrs Greville, who
was a friend of Queen Mary.

Elizabeth *Albert*

april 26th – May 7th

Above: The visit of Kaiser Wilhelm II (an intimate friend of Mrs Bankes) to Kingston Lacy in 1907. The children's governess, Miss Tidmarsh, (on the left, second row, wearing a hat trimmed with large cabbage roses) managed to insinuate herself into the group and was dismissed as soon as this was noticed in the photograph.

Below: The 10th Earl of Stamford and his mother with Haile Selassie, the exiled Emperor of Ethiopia, and the Crown Prince at Dunham Massey, Cheshire, in 1938.

Above: Guests arriving by motor car at Saltram in Devon in *c.* 1920. They were the guests of the 4th Earl of Morley.

Right: Lord Armstrong with Chinese visitors at Cragside, Northumberland, in 1911.

The Prime Minister, Stanley Baldwin (right), on a visit to Rudyard Kipling, 1923, while Kipling was living at Bateman's, East Sussex. Baldwin and Kipling were cousins.

Charlie Chaplin with Winston Churchill at
Chartwell, Kent, in 1931, the year Chaplin's
film *City Lights* came out.

Left: A house party at Montacute, Somerset, given in June 1905 for their daughter Clare by Constance, the wife of William Robert Phelips, the older man on the left of the group.

Below: Ernest Thesiger, the heart and soul of the house party, striking a pose for the camera once again. The photographs are from an album that belonged to one of the guests.

Above: Ernest Thesiger painting with members of the house party looking on. Before making his name as an actor, Thesiger studied at the Slade School of Fine Art with the intention of becoming an artist.

Above: Members of the Phelips family, and their relations the Ponsonbys, photographed at Montacute during cricket week 1905. William Robert Phelips and Molly Ponsonby are both holding box cameras.

Right: In conga formation, Countess of Albemarle, the daughter of the Earl Egerton, and guests at a house party at Tatton Park, Cheshire, in October 1901.

Above: Charles Paget Wade, *c.* 1925. He liked to dress up in the old costumes he had collected and would invite his visitors to Snowshill Manor, Gloucestershire, to take part in theatrical performances.

Left: Diana Massingberd and Susan Lushington in 1892. Both gifted musicians, they performed at Gunby Hall, Lincolnshire, and at the local festival inaugurated by Emily Langton Massingberd in nearby Skegness.

A scene from *Where there's a Will there's a Play*, a melodrama by the 'combined Tatton talent' with 'scenic effects and costumes by The Lady Egerton of Tatton', performed in 1891.

HISTORIC COSTUME BALL AT TATTON,

DECEMBER 10th, 1897.

DUCHESS OF BUCKINGHAM AND CHANDOS as Catarina Cornaro,
Queen of Cyprus.

EARL EGERTON OF TATTON as the Doge Morosini.

Left: The Duchess of Buckingham and Chandos and Earl Egerton dressed for a costume ball at Tatton Park in December 1897, the year Lord Egerton received an earldom. The Duchess had married the Earl as his second wife in 1894.

Right: The 5th Marquess of Anglesey in costume in *c*. 1900. Known as 'Toppy', he lived a life of fantasy and excess. He converted the chapel at Plas Newydd, Anglesey, into a theatre and put on private theatricals in which he took the leading role.

Household Servants

Census returns, household accounts and photographs record the numbers, and sometimes the names, of the servants. Indoor servants were classified as 'upper' and 'lower'. At meal times in the servants' hall they would be seated according to rank, and visiting servants according to the rank of their employers. After the meat course, the upper servants would leave in stately procession to eat their dessert in the housekeeper's room.

The butler – or house steward in a grand house – was responsible for the footmen and the male staff, while the housekeeper supervised the female staff down to the lowliest scullery maid. The cook, or chef, was counted among the upper servants, as were the valet and the lady's maid, who took care of their master and mistress's clothes respectively, helped them to dress and accompanied them when they were away from home. Status was reflected in the servants' wages and in their privileges and perquisites, known as 'perks'.

In photographs the butler looks older than the other menservants and, unlike the footmen, is not in livery. The housekeeper, who in recognition of her position was known as 'Mrs' regardless of whether she was married or single, wears a dark-coloured dress. While the footmen and maids slept two or three to a room – usually reached by separate staircases – the cook and housekeeper had their own bedrooms. The butler slept downstairs close to his pantry, the wine cellar and the safe containing the family plate.

Marriage between the servants was not uncommon, and several generations of the same family would work at the big house. George and Arthur Paddon, footmen at Cotehele in Cornwall at the turn of the century, were the sons of John Francis Paddon, the butler, and his wife Alice, the cook/housekeeper – and there was remarkable continuity at Erddig in Wales, where some of the staff spent all their working lives in the service of the Yorkes, gradually making their way into senior positions. Lucy Hitchman (who would marry Ernest Jones, the groom) came to work in the nursery as a young girl and in due course became the housekeeper.

The master and mistress of Erddig were particularly close to their servants and treated them well. The Yorkes had a long tradition of recording the people they employed, first in painted portraits which were hung on the walls of the servants' hall and later in photographs and doggerel verse. Kindness was almost always repaid with loyalty and tireless hard work.

The indoor staff at Cragside, Northumberland, in 1886. Andrew Crozier, the manservant on the left, came as a page boy in 1881 and would eventually become the butler. Cragside, built for the 1st Lord Armstrong, contained the latest technology. Electric lighting was installed, and an electric lift and dishwasher, all of great benefit to the servants.

A group of the Brownlows' servants at Ashridge Park, Hertfordshire, in *c.*
1870. The upper servants are seated in the middle of the photograph.

Above: Servants at Baddesley Clinton,
Warwickshire, in *c.* 1885. A Catholic
household, the servants joined the
family for prayers each evening at 9pm,
and on Wednesdays a priest came to
say Mass in the chapel.

Right: Servants at Chastleton House,
Oxfordshire, in *c.* 1910. Jane Millar, seated
with a cat on her lap, would later marry Jesse
Gardner who worked on the estate. Between
1897 and 1920 the house was let by the
Whitmore-Jones family to Charles Taswell
Richardson, a retired tea planter.

Far left: A group of servants at Kingston Lacy, Dorset, with a dog and a cat in *c.* 1920. Mrs Jenks ('Jenkes') was the housekeeper, Julia and Ellen, sisters from Ireland, were laundry maids, Ernest was a footman and Bessie Paine a kitchen maid.

Left: John Paddon, butler at Cotehele in Cornwall, his wife Alice, who was cook/housekeeper, and their daughter Alice, known as 'May', in *c.* 1898.

Below: The seventeen servants, including eight menservants, who worked for the Mount Edgcumbes at Cotehele, Cornwall, in 1906. In the centre of the group are Mr and Mrs Paddon.

Annie Gerry, a lady's maid at Dyrham Park,
Gloucestershire, and Dandy the dog in 1905.

Mrs Gibson, housekeeper at Lyme Park, Cheshire, seated in the courtyard, *c.* 1865.

Mary Webster, housekeeper at Erddig, Wrexham, in the mid-nineteenth century. A bunch of keys hangs from her hand indicating her office, which included responsibility for handing out the stores.

Above: Servants at Erddig in 1912, holding objects identifying them with their work. Lucy Hitchman, the nurse, in the second row on the left, holds a pair of children's shoes. In the window are Simon and Philip Yorke (the last of the family to live at Erddig) and their parents.

Right: Walter Read, a footman at Petworth House, West Sussex, photographed by Walter Kevis in 1905. Before setting up as a photographer and tobacconist in Petworth, Kevis had himself been employed as a footman at Petworth House.

Left: The laundry at Petworth House, West Sussex, *c.* 1889. Laundry maids generally lived locally and came in by the day. The man on the left is Reuben Hill, the 'odd man' who did the heavier jobs.

Frederick Leyland's butler, John Codling, and footmen posing in front of a buffet set up in the courtyard at Speke Hall, Liverpool, c.1870. Leyland rented the house from the Watt family.

Above: A group of Mrs Greville's servants photographed at Polesden Lacey, Surrey, in the 1920s. The man, Mr Wesley, was the third chauffeur. The maid on the right wearing a cap was the stillroom maid.

Right: Menservants at Polesden Lacey in c. 1928. From left to right: Mr Bole, house steward; Mr Smith, head chauffeur; Mr Moss, head butler; Mr Bacon, butler; and Mr Tell, valet. Bacon, a stout, rubicund figure, was known to help himself to the wine and food.

The chef and menservants photographed
in the conservatory at Tatton Park,
Cheshire, c. 1890. At the end of the
nineteenth century about 40 indoor servants
were employed by the Egertons.

MEAT SAFE LYME HALL

Monsieur Perez, the chef, and Mr Morten, the shepherd-cum-butcher, inspecting lamb carcases in the meat store at Lyme Park, *c*. 1910.

The kitchen staff at Waddesdon Manor, Buckinghamshire, where entertaining was on a lavish scale. They were photographed in 1910, when Alice de Rothschild, sister of Baron Ferdinand de Rothschild owned the house.

A kitchen maid at Ightham Mote, Kent, in the 1920s, a photograph taken
in the kitchen with a view through the mullioned windows.

Children of the House

'Children should be seen and not heard' was the attitude to boys and girls brought up in country houses in Victorian times. With clean clothes and well-brushed hair, they were sent downstairs by their nurse to be with the grown-ups for a few minutes after tea and before bed. They were to make no noise in the house and when visitors were present speak only when spoken to. The mistress of the house was expected to produce a son and heir, but once she had done so the children were regarded simply as appendages whose existence should not interfere with their parents' lives. Many pictures of these children were taken by professional photographers and show them beautifully dressed and the models of good behaviour they were supposed to be.

The most important person to them in the early years was the nurse, or nanny, who was photographed with her charges or on her own. She was either the most loving and comforting person they would ever know or a martinet in the nursery, as hard on the nursemaids as on the children.

Education began in the schoolroom with a governess. Some families had a succession of them, for various reasons; Miss Tidmarsh, governess to the Bankes children at Kingston Lacy in Dorset, disgraced herself during a visit from the King (see page 52) and was dismissed. Governesses were often French or German and for them it could be a difficult job to be in a large house in a foreign country, charged with teaching children disinclined to learn their language. Tutors were employed for boys who were not sent away to boarding schools, which by the late nineteenth century were also being founded for girls.

Children are shown in photographs with their donkeys and ponies, riding, driving pony carts, and in Northern Ireland, a cart drawn by a goat. They appear with their favourite toys, at the seaside, playing in the snow, on picnics and at birthday or fancy dress parties. A dog, cat or some more unusual pet is sometimes included in the pictures.

Fun seems to have come into children's lives, a trend that emerges in the books that were by then being written for and about children, especially in the early twentieth century. By 1926, when *Winnie the Pooh* was published, the desire to entertain children was paramount and what has been called 'the century of the child' was under way.

Lord Grey of Groby and Lady Jane Grey on the lawn at Dunham Massey, Cheshire, in 1906. Lord Grey was born in 1896. As 10th Earl of Stamford, he would die unmarried in 1976, the last of his line, and leave Dunham Massey to the National Trust.

Meinertzhagen children with their nurse at Mottisfont, Hampshire, in the 1890s. Daniel and Georgina Meinertzhagen took Mottisfont on a lease from the then owner, Mrs Vaudrey. Their ten children were brought up there.

Above: William John Watson-Armstrong and his sister Winifreda at Cragside, Northumberland, with their nurse. William was born in 1892 and Winifreda in 1894. Their father would inherit Cragside in 1900 from his great-uncle, Lord Armstrong, the great Victorian industrialist and builder of the house.

Right: The Hon. George Vernon aged four with his hoop. The photograph was taken at Sudbury Hall, the family seat in Derbyshire, in 1858.

Above: Walter Nugent and his German tutor
Herr Zimmerman at Castle Ward, Co. Down.
Walter was the son of Major Andrew Nugent who
in 1841 married the widow of Viscount Bangor.

Right: Mademoiselle Huguenin, a French governess
employed to teach the children at Castle Ward. This
and the photograph of the tutor were taken by Mary
Ward's brother-in-law William John Ward in 1861.

Mademoiselle Huguenin

The Hon. Mary Vere Agar-Robartes, born in 1879, the eldest of the ten Agar-Robartes children brought up at Lanhydrock, Cornwall, photographed with a puppy in *c.* 1892.

The Hon. Everilda Agar-Robartes, born in 1880, photographed with a cat in *c.* 1892. Everilda was the twin of Thomas, the eldest son of Lord Robartes (later Viscount Clifden) who fought in the Battle of Loos and was killed in battle in 1915.

Right: Five of the ten Agar-Robartes children bicycling in the gardens at Lanhydrock, *c.* 1896. From left to right: Violet, Constance, Gerald, Everilda and Thomas.

Above: The four youngest Agar-Robartes children in a carriage outside Lanhydrock in *c.*1898. From left to right: Violet, Constance, Alexander and Cecil.

Right: Right William John Watson-Armstrong on a tricycle in *c.* 1897. He would grow up in Northumberland at Bamburgh Castle and at Cragside, which would come to the National Trust in 1977, five years after his death.

Ralph Bankes, with his mother, reclining in a deck chair at Kingston
Lacy, Dorset. Born in 1902, Ralph was the spoilt only son of Henrietta
and Walter Bankes. During Nanny Stanley's reign in the nursery Ralph
was half-starved so that he was weak and dependent on her.

Summer for the Bankes children from Kingston Lacy was always spent at nearby Studland beach on the Corfe Castle estate, which also belonged to the Bankes family. Daphne, Viola and Ralph were photographed there in *c.* 1907.

Above: Viscount Valletort with his dog. Born in 1865, he was the younger brother of the Lady Victoria, Lady Albertha and Lady Edith Edgcumbe, and heir to the 4th Earl of Mount Edgcumbe.

Right: The Hon. Phyllis and the Hon. Hilda Legh with the mastiff Lady at Lyme Park, Cheshire, c. 1905. Lady was the last Lyme mastiff as Lord Newton did not approve of pet dogs and thought dogs should work.

Airmyne riding a donkey with her brother Henry beside her, a photograph taken at Calke Abbey, Derbyshire, in *c.* 1925. They were the grandchildren of Sir Vauncey Harpur-Crewe. Henry would be the last member of the family to live at Calke.

Richard Dyke Acland aged two, with his mother Eleanor and a donkey, in the park at Killerton, Devon, in 1908.

Meinertzhagen children: Barbara with Lawrencina and
Frederick in a goat cart, a photograph taken at
Mottisfont in 1890.

Georgina Elizabeth 'Betty', born in 1892, was the
youngest child of Daniel and Georgina Meinertzhagen.
She was photographed at Mottisfont, where she grew up,
in 1896.

Lady Mairi Vane
Tempest Stewart in a
goat cart at Mount
Stewart, Co. Down.
The youngest child of
the Marquess and
Marchioness of
Londonderry, she was
photographed with her
parents in 1923.

Daniel, the son of Daniel and Georgina Meinertzhagen, *c.* 1900. As boys growing up at Mottisfont, Daniel and his brother Richard were both passionate ornithologists.

The eagle cage was built for the Meinertzhagen boys against the side of the walled garden at Mottisfont. Adams is the bird keeper in the photograph, the dogs were named Pita and Vich.

The Dyke Acland brothers, Richard, Cuthbert and Geoffrey, in a hammock at Killerton in 1913. Cuthbert, known as 'Cubby', would be well known for his work as the National Trust Agent in the Lake District.

Agar-Robartes boys playing cricket on the lawn by the main entrance at Lanhydrock in *c.* 1896: Alexander batting and Cecil wicket-keeping.

Four of the five daughters of the Marquess of Anglesey: Lady Caroline, Lady Elizabeth, Lady Mary and Lady Rose Paget. They were photographed wearing dungarees in age and height order at home at Plas Newydd, Anglesey, in the 1920s.

Lady Ann and Lady Frances Cole, daughters of the Earl of Enniskillen, standing at the front door of Florence Court, Co. Fermanagh, dressed to go and feed the pigs. The photograph was taken in the mid-1920s.

Children taking part in a pageant, a photograph found at Calke Abbey, Derbyshire. Richard Harpur-Crewe, son of Sir Vauncey, had a small hand printing press at Calke on which he printed programmes for the theatrical performances which he and his sisters gave in the 1890s.

Estates and Gardens

A great country estate was largely self-sufficient. Overseeing the running of it was the agent, or estate manager, who was responsible for the maintenance of all the buildings, the letting of farms and the monitoring of the tenants. He was also responsible for the management of the Home Farm, which supplied meat, flour, milk and eggs to the big house and which might serve as an example of progressive farming methods to the tenants. The woods, sawmill, timber yard, estate workshops, wagon sheds, carpenter's shop and smithy all came under the watchful eye of the agent, as did the gardens.

Frequently, successive generations of an estate worker's family would be employed by the landowner. Their children would attend a school which had often been built by the family and where the mistress or daughters of the house sometimes assisted the schoolmaster or schoolmistress. Each summer the children of tenants and estate workers would be invited to tea in the garden of the big house. At Christmas they would go with their parents to a party at which everyone received a gift. The father might be given a new suit and a joint of beef or some game, the mother a length of cloth. On Sundays they would attend the church which might have been built or restored by the landowner's family, who also worshipped there.

The walled garden provided vegetables and fruit all the year round. In the bitter Northumberland winters not only grapes and peaches were grown in the glass houses at Wallington but avocado pears, guavas and pineapples. Produce was supplied to the big house while the family was in residence, normally from early autumn until the end of January, or packed in hampers for delivery to London – by train, once the railway had been extended.

A head gardener's reputation was founded on his ability to grow the new and exotic plants brought back by plant hunters to the leading nurseries each year. These exciting discoveries helped establish gardening as a fashionable occupation for landowners. Ludwig Messel grew plants from all over the world and hybridised new ones at Nymans in West Sussex from 1895. Vita Sackville-West, with the help of her husband Harold Nicolson, created the hugely influential garden at Sissinghurst in Kent among the crumbling red-brick walls of the old Tudor castle she bought in 1930.

The massed ranks of the tenants and estate staff employed by the Marquess of Bristol lined up in front of the Rotunda at Ickworth, Suffolk, in 1871.

Granny Baker, who occupied the lodge at Killerton, Devon, rent-free on condition that she opened the gate when she heard the coachman's whistle, *c.* 1890. The comparatively light duties of opening and shutting the gates were frequently given to a retired member of staff.

Beer was brewed at Lyme Park, Cheshire, until 1914, with the gamekeeper Jim Shufflebotham in charge. The Old Ale had a fearful reputation for its strength.

Above: Fred King, Frank Hardy and Fred Moss in the carpenter's shop at Dyrham Park, Gloucestershire, in 1906. An estate carpenter was required to turn his hand to anything from the construction of smaller buildings and re-roofing of estate cottages to repairing and making furniture, and even the construction of stage sets.

Right: The saw-pit at Gunby Hall, Lincolnshire, in 1935. The estate of almost 1,500 acres with fifteen farms was still reliant on its steam-driven saw-mill for all the timber used on the estate and to provide a surplus for sale.

Margaret Lushington with a prize sheep. She would marry
Stephen Massingberd of Gunby Hall in 1898.

Sheep shearing. Joe Morten was the shepherd at Lyme Park from 1898 to 1904. In spring all hands would be called on to help with the shearing.

Harvesting in 1889 on the Arlington Court estate in Devon. Advanced estates such as Woburn Abbey in Bedfordshire had introduced steam threshing machines as early as 1804, but such innovations took a long time to reach a remote north Devon estate.

Gamekeepers on the Speke estate near Liverpool in *c.*1905.

Above: Mr Kidwell, the gamekeeper at Arlington Court, Devon. Sir Bruce Chichester was an enthusiastic sportsman. Not so his daughter who, on inheriting, banned first hunting and later shooting on the estate.

Right: The ferret man with his terriers at Ickworth, *c.* 1930. Controlling the rabbit population was a major undertaking on most estates. Ferrets were kept by the keepers and sent down the burrows to flush out the rabbits.

Class for natural History . 1890

A natural history class at Arlington Court in 1890. Many wives and daughters of landowners helped out in the village school. Miss Rosalie Chichester taught the children of her tenants her own favourite subject.

Lady Phyllis Hervey and the Scouts at Ickworth. The Scout movement, inaugurated in 1907, was quickly welcomed by many landowners, who provided a place for summer camps on their land.

Boys' football team at Stourhead, Wiltshire, *c.* 1900, with Harry Hoare in the centre of the photograph. This was a rare opportunity for the children of the estate and the house to play together.

Left: Two of the gardeners ready to bat for Ickworth, c. 1910.

Below: Fred Gibson, head gardener, taking the middle stump for Lyme Park, Cheshire, c. 1890. Lyme had its own cricket team, cricket pitch (lovingly looked after by the garden staff and reckoned as good as any county ground) and pavilion. When advertising for new staff it was emphasized that cricketers were preferred.

Ice gatherers at Clumber Park, Nottinghamshire, in *c.* 1905. In a hard winter, when the lake froze solid, large blocks of ice would be cut to fill the ice-house. When well packed, the ice would keep for more than two years.

The Duke of Newcastle almost bankrupted himself on the construction of his chapel at Clumber, designed by G.F. Bodley. It had its own choir school. The photograph dates from *c.* 1905.

The head gardener at Lyme Park was in charge of a large team which included several 'dirty men' to stoke the boilers for the glasshouses. There were two vineries, a Malmaison house (carnations), two cucumber houses and a melon house, as well as three hot-houses to produce the stove-plants required to decorate the house, summer and winter. A photograph of *c.* 1900.

Robert Sale, head gardener at Ickworth on the left of a group of assistant gardeners photographed in *c.* 1899. The head gardener had a handsome house while his unmarried assistants lived together in the bothy.

Sellick, gardener at Saltram, Devon, with a prize hydrangea in 1895. A head gardener was judged on his ability to propagate the exotic cultivars imported from China and America.

Mary Gatecliff was in charge of the walled garden at Attingham Park, Shropshire, from 1941 to 1944. The garden supplied vegetables for the house and local air base, and any surplus was sold in the market in Shrewsbury.

The 3rd Earl of Morley constructing the fern garden at Saltram, *c.* 1890. He and his wife *née* Margaret Holford, daughter of the creator of Westonbirt Arboretum, came to Saltram in 1884 and set about planting the garden with exotic trees and shrubs. The boy on the rockery is their younger son Montagu.

Left: Churchill building a garden wall at Chartwell, Kent, with the help of his daughter Sarah in 1928.

Right: Colonel Leonard Messel and his head gardener, Mr Comber, at Nymans, West Sussex, in the 1940s. Comber started as a garden boy at Nymans in 1895 and retired in 1953.

Left: Mr Burnett in the 1930s constructing the armature for the topiary huntress for the Shamrock Garden at Mount Stewart, Co. Down, part of the Marchioness of Londonderry's inspired design for the gardens.

Far right: Ulric Hopkins and a banana tree, 1906. Ulric was the son of Edric Hopkins, the first owner of Sharpitor (Overbeck's) in Devon. In the semi-tropical garden exotics grew happily outdoors.

Celebrations and Disasters

Families being welcomed home by their servants and tenants after an absence abroad, and particularly on bringing a new bride to the family house, are events frequently recorded in photographs. Such events were a largely nineteenth-century re-creation of Merrie Englande, designed to bind the tenants to the family by ties of shared memory. However, for the family as well as the estate, the most significant event was the coming of age of the heir. This birthday was celebrated by the family, the estate, the neighbours and the county, with feasting on a gargantuan scale for days together. The tenants and staff would present a piece of silver bearing a suitable inscription, and the villages, gates and lodges of the whole estate would be decorated.

The wedding of the daughter of the house was celebrated in similar fashion. The style of the wedding dress, bouquet, veil and garland had been popularised by Queen Victoria's wedding and was emulated right down the social scale. A newly married couple arriving at the family home for the first time would have their horses unhitched from the carriage and a party of men from the estate would pull it up the drive to the decorated house while the church bells pealed. Lower-key events frequently included an annual flower and vegetable show followed perhaps by a cricket match, children's tea and tenants' dinner and dance.

National events such as Queen Victoria's Golden and Diamond Jubilees, royal weddings and victories abroad were celebrated. In tragedy too the whole estate came together. The terrible losses of the First World War were commemorated with memorials on village greens and in churches, unveiled at ceremonies attended by the whole community.

Country houses were always at risk of fire. Wood panelling and flammable furniture and textiles made a house lit by candles, heated by open fires, and with meat spit-roasted in the kitchen, a tinderbox. As the houses stood alone in their parks, far from help, a fire engine was present on most estates and men from the estate were provided with uniforms and served as firemen. The number of country houses lost to fires demonstrates how necessary it was to take these precautions, and sometimes how inadequate they were. Some houses seem to have been particularly unlucky; both Cliveden in Buckinghamshire and Clumber Park in Nottinghamshire were burnt three times, and the latter was eventually demolished in 1938.

The coming-of-age celebrations for the Hon. Thomas Wodehouse Legh in 1878. The celebrations lasted for days with feasting, dancing and fireworks and were attended by the local gentry and all the people on the Lyme Park estate in Cheshire.

Above: Lady Adelaide Chetwynd-Talbot, youngest daughter of the Earl of Shrewsbury, and Earl Brownlow at Ashridge Park on their engagement in 1868. They enjoyed almost 50 years together, though unblessed by children.

Right: Stephen Massingberd, a model landlord, dutiful and cultivated, married the beautiful and talented Margaret Lushington. They were photographed in the garden at Gunby Hall, Lincolnshire, in 1898.

Left: The wedding of Beatrice Luard-Selby and Alfred Willink in April 1885, a photograph taken in the courtyard at Ightham Mote, Kent.

Right: Annie Gerry's wedding on 25 April 1906 to Wallace Rumney. Both were employed at Dyrham Park, Gloucestershire. Annie, the niece of Miss Saunders (companion to Mrs Blathwayt), was a lady's maid and Wallace Rumney an apprentice carpenter.

Lord and Lady Rodney welcomed back to Berrington Hall, Herefordshire, by the estate and staff after their honeymoon in 1891. The house and gates were decorated with bunting, their carriage was pulled up the drive by tenants, who presented a gift of silver, and all were entertained at a garden party.

The Hon. Piers Legh and his wife Sarah (*née* Polk Bradford) during their honeymoon at Lyme Park, Cheshire, in 1920. Sarah's first husband, Captain the Hon. Alfred Shaughnessy, had been killed in action in 1916.

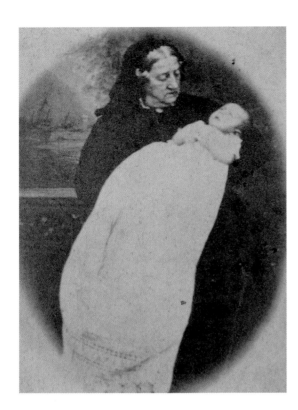

Left: The christening of Robert Blathwayt in 1850. He was photographed in the arms of his grandmother, Marianne Vesey. Robert would inherit Dyrham Park in 1899.

Far right: The family of Julius Drewe photographed at Castle Drogo, Devon, at the time of the christening of Margaret (born 1930), the daughter of Beatrice and Cedric Drewe.

Right: James and Margaret Beale with their seven children and first grandchild at Standen, West Sussex, in 1902.

Ralph Bankes's coming of age in 1923. The celebrations at
Kingston Lacy, Dorset, followed the same lines as those for
his father 50 years earlier and included the presentation of
silver by the estate staff.

The 3rd Lord Sackville's funeral cortège passing through the park at Knole, Kent, in 1928. Retainers followed on foot at the back of the procession while members of the family, apart from the men immediately behind the carriage, travelled by motor car.

The Marchioness of Bristol at a children's party at
Ickworth, Suffolk, to mark the coronation of George V
in 1911. She wore her coronation robes and each
child was presented with a commemorative mug.

On the left, Sir Henry Hoare of Stourhead, Wiltshire, at an agricultural show in *c.* 1905. He was an expert on horses and bred Percheron draft horses himself. He often served as a judge at shows.

The annual Agricultural Show at Clumber Park in Nottinghamshire with the Duchess of Newcastle presenting the prizes in 1906.

Above: A rally at Stourhead of the Conservative Working Men's Benefit Society, Wiltshire branch, in 1908. A non-political insurance scheme, the society provided support to its subscribers when they were unable to work through ill-health. The Hoares were keen supporters.

Right: Lloyd George with Sir Francis Dyke Acland at Killerton, Devon, in 1925. Although originally Tories, the Aclands moved steadily left, first supporting the Liberal party. Eventually Sir Richard Acland tried to sell his estates to fund a more radical party of his own.

Maypole dancing at a garden fête at Attingham Park, Shropshire, in
1924, one of the revivals of the English Folk Song and Dance Society
supported by Lady Berwick.

Tea in the stable yard at Chastleton House, Oxfordshire. By the 1930s the annual village fête held in the grounds of a big house to raise funds for the church was all that remained of the great estate entertainments.

The spectacle of the Great Barn at Knole burning in August 1887. The estate would turn out to fight a fire, but with poor equipment and insufficient water often little could be done to save a building.

Stourhead on 16 April 1902, the morning after the fire, which was vainly fought by engines from three neighbouring estates as well as the town engines from Frome and Mere. A well-organised team of staff managed to evacuate the principal rooms, saving most of the famous collections.

Outdoor Pursuits

Though he might spend part of the year enjoying the social life of London or participating in national affairs, the owner of a large estate was usually a countryman at heart. He loved horses and dogs, which played a large part in the sporting activities that brought him close to nature and to his tenants, the people who worked his land.

Of all the field sports, foxhunting was the most popular. By the 1880s more than 10,000 people of all ages went out hunting – the women riding side-saddle – with almost the same number following on foot. In West Sussex at the end of the nineteenth century the Leconfield Hunt, of which Lord Leconfield was both owner and master, met six days a week. The kennels were on the edge of the park at Petworth and the stables close to the house. The army of men looking after the hunters and carriage-horses included grooms, coachmen, farriers and stable lads.

Edward VII's love of foxhunting was overtaken in the latter part of his life by a passion for shooting, which was also the principal occupation of the son who would succeed him as George V. Where royalty led, others with land and money followed. The ladies would stand – or sit on shooting-sticks – with the guns, and there were some who took part in the shoot themselves. A hearty lunch would be laid on in a lodge or barn while the keepers, loaders and beaters ate separately.

Fishing was the third major field sport pursued by country gentlemen. The river Test, which runs crystal-clear through the Mottisfont estate in Hampshire, was one of the best rivers for dry-fly fishing and for enjoying the peace of the countryside.

Golf became popular in the last years of the nineteenth century. The putting green at Knightshayes Court in Devon was created as a gift to Sir John Heathcoat-Amory and his wife, who, as Joyce Wethered, had been the English Ladies Golf Champion. Cricket matches were played against local teams and friends, and cricketing families would organise a whole week of games.

In the 1920s lawn tennis became a more popular game for women, playing together or in mixed doubles; croquet and bowls were for the less energetic. A bicycle – or tricycle – ride was a fashionable outdoor activity, more enjoyable when a party of people set off together. Meanwhile, at houses situated close to water there was swimming, boating and outings to the beach.

A lawn-meet at Attingham Park, Shropshire, in *c.* 1925, with a man drinking a stirrup-cup and ladies riding side-saddle.

N° 3

The stable yard at Petworth House, West Sussex, a photograph taken in 1887 of the men who looked after the hunters and carriage-horses for Lord Leconfield. The men's living quarters were on the first floor of the building.

opening meet of Tiverton Foxhounds at Knightshayes.

Sir John Heathcoat-Amory, 1st Bart, photographed in 1911 in the porch of Knightshayes Court, the house he had built for him in Devon. Dressed for hunting are, on the left, his eldest son Ian and Charles Carew (married to his eldest daughter), on the right, his sons Ludovic (who would die in 1918 from wounds received in action) and Harry.

Sir Ian Heathcoat-Amory, 2nd Bart, with his wife Alexandra at Knightshayes Court in *c.* 1925. He was master of the Tiverton Foxhounds and would die in 1931 from a fall out hunting. He was the breeder of Tiverton Actor, a famous stallion hound.

Above: Moving off. Horses, hounds and followers in a horse-drawn carriage and motor car at Stourton, a village on the Stourhead estate, Wiltshire, in *c.* 1910.

Right: Robert Wynter Blathwayt out with the Beaufort Hunt in the park at Dyrham, Gloucestershire, in *c.* 1925. Among the followers are his wife Margaret, and his daughters and their nurse.

Terrier men on the Stourhead estate in *c.* 1910.

The Barrington Beagles outside Barrington Court, Somerset, in 1936. From left to right: Julia Lyle; her husband Ian Lyle, the huntsman; Captain Beacham, the Lyles' agent; Elsie 'Ronnie' Lyle, the widow of Colonel Arthur Lyle, who had rescued the house, and her daughters Barbara and Joan.

Above: James Worsley Pennyman shouldering a gun on the left and his younger brother Alfred Worsley Pennyman on the right, in the stable yard at Ormesby Hall, North Yorkshire, in 1885.

Left: After a rabbit shoot at Arlington Court, Devon, c. 1860. Sir Bruce Chichester with his keeper (and butler in the background) in front of the house before it was extended.

'Bringing in the Birds' a photograph taken at a duck shoot at Lyme Park, Cheshire, in *c.* 1912.

Keepers and beaters at the 3rd Earl of Morley's shoot on the Saltram estate in Devon, a photograph taken in 1894.

The Earl of Morley and his shooting party at Plymbridge Cottage on the Saltram estate in 1895. The Earl points to the pheasants on the ground.

Anglers equipped with rods, nets and creels for a day's fishing on the Test, the chalk river which runs through the Mottisfont estate in Hampshire. Dry-fly fishing first became popular on the Test.

A mounted game of push ball at the Clumber Park Show in Nottinghamshire in 1906. The ball, approximately the height of a horse's breastbone, was pushed towards the goal by the horses, without being touched by the riders.

Above: Players and spectators at a cricket match at Lyme Park, Cheshire, in c. 1890. The young men with moustaches and wearing striped caps are the Hon. Thomas Legh and his brother the Hon. Gilbert Legh.

Right: Croquet at Knole in Kent in the 1850s. Watching is Mortimer Sackville-West, later 1st Lord Sackville.

Above: At Tyntesfield, Somerset, Antony Gibbs (second from the left) and members of his family balance, some precariously, on their bicycles. The photograph was taken in 1896.

Right: A cigarette-smoking tricyclist outside the main entrance of Cragside in Northumberland in *c.* 1897. Tricycles designed for grown-ups appeared in the 1880s.

An outing to the seaside. William Henry Watson-Armstrong with his son William John in *c.* 1897. William Henry would be created Lord Armstrong of Bamburgh and Cragside in 1903.

A bathing party from Florence Court, Co. Fermanagh, at Loch Erne, photographed in the mid-1920s. Lady Frances Cole is second from the left and Lady Ann Cole second from the right.

Travelling

Travelling by road in Britain at the start of the nineteenth century was uncomfortable, expensive and frequently dangerous. Most roads were built and maintained by the parish, the work entrusted to labourers without the benefit of a surveyor or engineer. Turnpike roads were little better and yet costly to use – coaches paid 6d per mile to travel on them.

Small wonder, then, that alternative means of transport were eagerly sought. Following the enormously successful opening of the Liverpool to Manchester route in 1830, railway mania took hold. By the 1850s there were over 10,460km (6,500 miles) of railway in Britain, and with fares a third of the cost of those charged by stage coaches, the train was causing a revolution in travel. Travel was no longer the prerogative of the wealthy: train excursions to the seaside, weekend stays at country houses, and even a home in the country at a commutable distance from the office, were achievable goals for many middle-class families.

Meanwhile, carriage construction was enjoying a revolution. The high perch with the huge wheels and the four in hand, which had been made fashionable by the Carlton House Set, required strength and skill on the part of the driver. These were giving way to carriages that provided greater comfort for the traveller.

A new and egalitarian form of transport appeared in the 1870s – bicycling. However, the so-called 'penny farthing' was dangerous on account of its height and it was not until the invention of the small-wheeled 'safety bicycle' that the sport became suitable for all riders – though it was Dunlop's pneumatic tyre, patented in 1888, that first provided a ride considered comfortable enough for ladies.

Yet an even greater transport revolution was on the horizon, and many early enthusiasts of the bicycle quickly switched their allegiance to the motor car. Pioneer motorists swathed themselves in dust coats, goggles and scarves to combat the clouds of dust they raised from unmade roads. A solution had to be found and asphalt was mixed with road chippings to make Tarmac, the ubiquitous black-top road surface that spread across England in the years immediately before the First World War.

Among the wealthy and adventurous, road transport was soon not enough. Maurice Egerton at Tatton was the owner of the first car registered in Cheshire, a 1900 Benz; just ten years later he had taken up flying and was a member of the Royal Aero Club, with certificate No. 11.

A canoe landau in the park at Clumber, Nottinghamshire, *c.* 1900. By the end of the nineteenth century carriage building in England had reached a peak of excellence, in both design and finish.

Left: The Sumner party in a park drag departing for Ascot races from Hatchlands Park, Surrey, in *c.* 1860. Such vehicles were popular for sporting events as the roof-top seats afforded excellent views of the action.

Right: Albinia Rose Gibbs of Tyntesfield, Somerset, driving a well-bottomed gig in *c.* 1895. Two-wheeled vehicles paid half the road duty of four-wheeled vehicles.

Left: Amalia Sackville-West in a *vis-à-vis* by the Great Gate at Knole, Kent, in the 1890s. Both Amalia and her sister Victoria Sackville-West (who married in 1890) lived at Knole from 1889 when their father became the 2nd Lord Sackville and inherited the estate.

Right: Samuel and Helen Beale in a dog cart at Standen, West Sussex, in *c.* 1894. This was a popular vehicle, with a large locker beneath the seat that was originally for carrying dogs to sporting events. It became the ubiquitous form of transport for the farmer and country doctor.

The Countess of Mount Edgcumbe, wife of the 5th Earl, taking a carriage drive on the Cotehele estate in Cornwall in *c.* 1920. By this date carriage driving was more a sport than a regular means of transport.

The 4th Earl of Morley being helped into his invalid carriage by Nurse Little and Stevens the butler at Saltram, Devon, in *c.* 1930. Watching, on the right, is the Hon. Lionel St Aubyn, Lord Morley's brother-in law.

The Marquess of Bristol and his coachman, Arkwright, departing
from Ickworth, Suffolk, for a drive in a pony park phaeton in 1907.
He was already ill and died on 7th August that year.

Harriet Rogers, the housekeeper, being driven, *c.*1895
in a four-wheeled donkey cart built at Erddig, Wrexham.
The cart was built at the property and can still be found in
the stable yard.

Left: Gerard and Clare Phelips in a Norfolk cart by the orangery at Montacute House in Somerset, *c.* 1900.

Right: A donkey sulky photographed at Cirencester polo ground by Maurice Egerton in *c.* 1905. Maurice became the 4th Lord Egerton of Tatton on his father's death in 1920.

Maurice Egerton in his 1900 Benz. This was the first car to be registered in Cheshire, with the number plate M1. (From 1903 all cars had to carry a number plate, each county having its own initial letter.) The Benz is in the garage at Tatton.

Sir Ian Heathcoat-Amory of Knightshayes Court, Devon, leaving the family's factory, John Heathcoat & Co., at Tiverton in *c.* 1901 to motor to Scotland. The vehicle was modelled on a Lanchester design, with a passenger seat in front of the driver.

Mrs Greville's chauffeurs and mechanics with her cars in the stable
courtyard at Polesden Lacey, Surrey, in the 1920s.

Chapman, the Beales' chauffeur, driving into the courtyard at Standen in 1904. Before they bought their first car, he had been the Beales' head coachman.

Larry, the Colyer-Fergusson's chauffeur, on the moat bridge at Ightham Mote, Kent, c.1920.

Lord and Lady Berwick with Rowe, the chauffeur, and the alsatians in Lady
Berwick's little Renault at Attingham Park, Shropshire, in c.1925.

Lady cyclist at Rufford Old Hall, Lancashire, in 1906. With the advent of the pneumatic tyre in 1888, and more particularly the safety bicycle in the 1890s, cycling became enormously popular.

Richard Harpur-Crewe preparing to fly from Brooklands, c. 1910. His father, Sir Vauncey, was passionately opposed to all aspects of modern life. His son, by contrast, was a pioneer motorist and pilot. He had to keep his car outside the park gates at Ticknall as Sir Vauncey would permit neither motor car nor bicycle inside the park at Calke Abbey, Derbyshire.

A gas balloon ascent *c.* 1909, photographed by Maurice Egerton of Tatton Park, a friend of the Short brothers who manufactured gas balloons.

Wartime

The most poignant photographs of all are perhaps those taken during the two World Wars. Men and boys are shown newly in uniform before going off to fight, images that would be much treasured in their absence. Among them are pictures of the fathers and sons, husbands and fiancés who would never come home.

With the men away, women coped on the Home Front. In the First World War they became auxiliary nurses, wearing starched white aprons, or cooks or drivers as members of the Voluntary Aid Detachment (VAD). In the Second World War they joined organisations such as the new Women's Voluntary Service (WVS) or the Women's Land Army: by 1944 over 80,000 Land Girls, brown-breeched and gumbooted, were working on farms and in market gardens.

Women were also employed in moving children to safe places in the country. Evacuees from the cities and refugees from countries under Nazi occupation were accommodated in country houses and in farmhouses and cottages on the estates. Classes with their teachers – and in some cases, entire schools – decamped to grand homes such as Hatchlands Park in Surrey, Scotney Castle in Kent and Nymans in West Sussex. After initial homesickness, some of the children had the time of their lives: boys from a school evacuated to Barrington Court in Somerset became enthusiastic followers of the Barrington Beagles. Very young children were given refuge at Lyme Park in Cheshire and Dyrham Park in Gloucestershire.

Some of the country houses now owned by the National Trust played a part in both wars. Knightshayes Court in Devon became a hospital in the First World War, then a convalescent home in the Second. In 1914 Waldorf Astor offered the bowling alley and tennis and fives courts at Cliveden in Buckinghamshire to the Canadian Red Cross as a site for what became the Duchess of Connaught Red Cross Hospital. This was partially rebuilt in 1940 for the same purpose. And in 1915 Overbeck's (then known as Sharpitor) in Devon became a hospital, while during the Second World War US soldiers were stationed there, using the garden for target practice.

At West Wycombe Park in Buckinghamshire, local women were supervised by Lady Dashwood in the 1940s as they did their bit for the war effort, knitting and making pyjamas and rag rugs. Part of the Wallace Collection was evacuated there and it was to West Wycombe that the National Trust office and staff retreated for safety at the beginning of the war, staying until January 1943.

Medical staff at Knightshayes Court, Devon, during the First World War. Lady Heathcoat-Amory, wife of Sir John, was matron of the hospital, in charge of discipline.

Convalescing First World War soldiers at Sharpitor (Overbeck's) in Devon. The house was offered to the Red Cross Society by Captain and Mrs Vereker after their son was killed in the retreat from Mons.

Soldiers playing billiards at Sharpitor (Overbeck's). The hospital was run entirely by VADs (members of the Voluntary Aid Detachment) between the years 1915 and 1919.

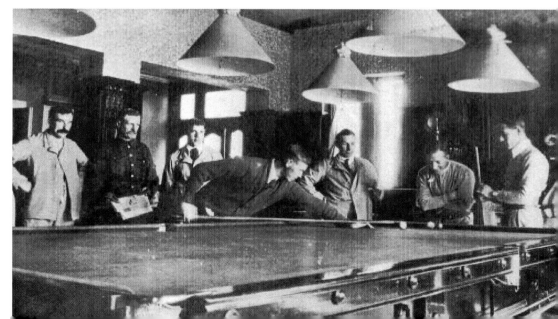

William Robbins, who worked on the Ickworth estate in Suffolk, photographed in army uniform in 1917.

During the First World War, Sydney Beale on home leave with his mother Margaret Beale in the garden of Standen in West Sussex.

Left: The Heathcoat-Amory family assembled at Knightshayes Court, Devon, during the Second World War, before Patrick and Gerald, on the left, were killed. Sitting on the left is Sir John 'Jack' Amory, whose wife Joyce (famous as the golfer Joyce Wethered) stands on the far right beside his brother William and, sitting on the right, his brother Roderick.

Right: American airmen in the grounds of Knightshayes Court, which was used as a US Air Force convalescent home in the Second World War. An American Mustang crashed in the wood in 1945, doing aerobatics, and the idea of creating a woodland garden began when the trees and debris were cleared.

The visit of Queen Elizabeth with Princess Elizabeth and Princess Margaret to the Canadian Red Cross Memorial Hospital during the Second World War. The hospital replaced one built in 1914 on land at Cliveden in Buckinghamshire offered by Waldorf Astor. His wife, Nancy Astor, is seated on the right.

Above: Forty children in all from Manchester were looked after by nurses at Lyme Park, Cheshire, during the Second World War.

Right: Children evacuated from London during the Second World War with their cots in the garden at Dyrham Park, Gloucestershire. The residential nursery was organised by Lady Islington, who had Dyrham Park on a lease from the Blathwayts.

Evacuee children with Nurse Watson at Lyme Park. Children were there throughout
the war with Lord Newton living mainly in the library with his dogs.

Pupils of St Anne's College, Sanderstead, at Hatchlands Park, Surrey, in 1940.
One of the girls was among the *Kinderchildren* who left Germany in a sealed
train and one of the two boys was a refugee living in the village.

King's School, Rochester, Junior School was evacuated to Scotney Castle in Kent between 1939 and 1940. Edward Windsor Hussey and his wife Rosamond are seated in the centre of the group.

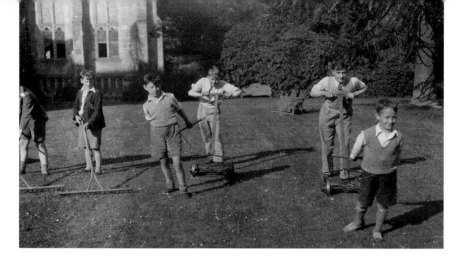

Above: Sixteen boys from the Buckingham Gate Central School in London were housed at Nymans, West Sussex, during the Second World War. They attended the local school, alternating with the local children so that each child spent only half a day there.

Right: As part of the war effort the evacuees, photographed in the woodshed at Nymans, helped with the drying of herbs from the garden.

Left: A gym class for children from Portsmouth High School for Girls who were moved to the safety of Hinton Ampner in Hampshire, requisitioned in the Second World War.

Below: The choir, photographed by Ralph Dutton, the owner of Hinton Ampner, on the school's open day in 1942.

Right: A performance of *The Pied Piper* by the High School girls at Hinton Ampner in 1942.

Joan Milne, a Land Girl, with Taffy Davies, the gardener from Lyme Park, Cheshire, at Green Close Farm on the estate in 1940.

Ploughing on the Holnicote estate, Somerset. Horses were brought back to save on the fuel needed to run tractors.

A working party of local women in the South Colonnade at West Wycombe Park,
Buckinghamshire, in 1941.

The National Trust moved to West Wycombe Park, Buckinghamshire, setting up its office in the Brown Drawing Room, where Miss Balachey, a typist and a junior aged 15 worked. James Lees-Milne was at West Wycombe when he was not touring the country in an old Austin on National Trust business.

Acknowledgements

We are extremely grateful for the help we have received from all the National Trust staff we have contacted in connection with this book. In particular we would like to thank:

Frances Bailey, Andrew Barber, Hugo Brown, Sophie Chessum, Philip Claris, Richard Dean, Charles Pugh and Emma Slocombe; Del Wiggins (Barrington Court), Rob Gray (Kingston Lacy), Demelza Parker-Williams (Arlington Court), Chloe Tapping (Scotney Castle), Hannah Holohan (Ightham Mote), Rachel Spiller (Hatchlands Park), Anna Pizzey (Mottisfont Abbey), Bryher Mason (Castle Drogo), Heather Ball (Coleton Fishacre), Rachel Hunt (Cotehele), Denise Melhuish (Killerton), Samantha Short (Overbeck's), Ben Shapcott (Saltram), Vicky Nutt (Polesden Lacey), Nicky Ingram (Standen), Rebecca Plumb (Hinton Ampner), Sonja Power (Montacute House), Toby Currant (Knightshayes Court), Rebecca Graham (Nymans), Amy Carney (Lyme Park), Caroline Schofield (Tatton Park), John Parkinson (Calke Abbey), David Fitzer (Belton House), Saraid Jones (Attingham Park), Karen Symonds and Andrew Sawyer (Cragside), Eleanor Ingle (Felbrigg Hall), Jim Chestnutt (Florence Court), Kate Yates (Ickworth), Paul Holden and Ginny Clotworthy (Lanhydrock), Liz Hayward (Ormesby Hall), Joy Tovey (Packwood House) and Ruth Moppett (Tyntesfield).

We hope that their interest in the photographs of the people who once lived and worked at the houses will be refreshed by the research they undertook on our behalf.

We would like to thank Alison McCann at West Sussex Record Office for her help over the Petworth House photographs and Rose Lock at Special Collections, University of Sussex, for her help over the photographs of Kipling at Bateman's; also Bridget Sackville-West for helping with the photographs at Knole Jonathan Wager for identifying members of the Beale family of Standen, Randle Meinertzhagen for putting us straight about his relations at Mottisfont Abbey and Lady Rose Lauritzen about hers at Mount Stewart, David Heathcoat-Amory for information about his family and Jenny Warrack for helping to select pictures from Kingston Lacy. Above all we would like to thank Lucy Smith at Anova Books for her infinite patience and diligence.

Picture Credits

Anova Books and the National Trust and National Trust (Enterprises) Ltd are committed to respecting the intellectual property rights of others. Reasonable efforts have been made to contact, identify and acknowledge copyright holders where applicable. Any copyright owner who may be incorrectly acknowledged or omitted should contact us so that any required corrections may be made.

Images © National Trust Images: Pages 14, 28, 29, 43, 44, 47, 54, 65, 71 (right), 75 (right), 78, 83 (right), 114; Page 35 © NTI/Cliff Guttridge; Pages 18 (right), 34, 41 (right), 49 (right), 87, 96 (right), 105 (left) (additional © Rosalie Chichester),124, 183, © NTI/ John Hammond; Page 58 ©NTI/Angelo Hornak; Page 70 © NTI/ A. Vesey; Page 39 © NTI/ John Wickens (additional © Estate of Rex Whistler. All rights reserved, DACS 2012); Page 52 (right) © NTI/ Mike Williams.

National Trust Images/Historic Properties Photographic Archive Collection: Pages 12 (Courtesy of Lord Sackville), 16, 17 (left), 18 (left), 20 (left), 21, 25 (right and left), 26 (right, Courtesy of Lord Sackville), 26 (left), 32, 33 (right, Courtesy of Lord Sackville), 36, 63, 73 (left), 75 (left), 81, 82 (Courtesy of Col. R. Meinertzhagen Estate), 110, 111, 117 (Earl of Rosse), 118 (Courtesy of Lady Mairi Bury Estate); 123 (left), 129 (Courtesy of Lord Sackville), 131 (right), 136 (Courtesy of Lord Sackville), 137, 142 (right), 146, 147, 149, 151 (Courtesy of Lord Sackville), 157, 160 (Courtesy of Lord Sackville), 164, 165 (left), 168, 187.

National Trust Property: Arlington Court: 8 (right), 103 (right, Rosalie Chichester), 106 (Rosalie Chichester), 144 (left); Ashdown House (David Watson): 13 (left); Attingham Park: 38,115 (left) 155 (left), 134, 139, 170; Baddesley Clinton: Page 19, 67 (left); Bateman's: 54; Barrington Court (Courtesy of Andrew Lyle): 143 (right); Belton House: 13 (right), 66, 122 (left); Calke Abbey: 91 (left), 97, 172; Castle Drogo: 17, 36, 127; Castle Ward: 8 (left, Mary Ward); 84 (William John Ward); Chastleton (David Watson): 67 (right, courtesy of Mrs Suzanne Folland), 135; Coleton Fishacre: 45; Cotehele: 162 (top) Courtesy of Earl of Mount Edgcumbe Collection: 2, 69, 90 (left); Cragside: 53 (right), 83 (left), 86 (right), 153, 154; Dyrham Park: 14, 126 (left), 180 (right); 101 (left, A.Vesey), 123 (right, A.Vesey); Felbrigg Hall: 23; Florence Court, (Courtesy of Lady Ann Cole Estate): 96 (left), 155; Gawthorpe Hall: 33 (left, Nina Kay-Shuttleworth); Gunby Hall (Robert Thrift): 17 (right), 60 (left), 101 (right), 102, 122 (right); Hatchlands Park: 182; Hinton Ampner: 185; Ickworth: 99, 105 (right), 107, 109 (left), 113, 130, 177 (left); Ightham Mote: 40, 79, 169 (right); Killerton (Courtesy of Dominic Acland): 20 (right), 91 (right), 95 (left), 100 (left), 133; Kingston Lacy: 49 (left), 52 (left), 68, 88, 89, 128; Knightshayes Court (Courtesy of Sir Ian Heathcoat-Amory): 141, 167, 175, 178 Lanhydrock: 85, 86 (left), 95 (right); Lyme Park: 71 (left), 77, 90 (right), 100 (right), 103 (left), 109 (right), 112, 121(Greater Manchester County Record Office), 125 (James Colville), 145, 150 (Greater Manchester County Record Office),180 (left), 181, 186; Mottisfont Abbey (Courtesy of Col. R. Meinertzhagen Estate): 148; Ormesby Hall: 144 (right); Overbeck's (Sharpitor): 119, 176; Polesden Lacey: 4, 50, 51(Illustrated London News); Rufford Old Hall: 171; Saltram: 53 (left), 115 (right), 162 (below); Scotney Castle: 31; Snowshill Manor: 42 (above), 60 (right); Speke Hall: 74, 104; Standen (Courtesy of Beale family): 37, 126, 161, 169 (left), 177 (right); Stourhead: 108, 131 (left), 132, 142 (left), 143 (left); Tatton Park (Cheshire East Council): 48, 59, 61, 62, 76, 165 (right), 166, 173; Tyntesfield: 22, 152, 159.

Other Collections:
Page 179 © Viscount Astor.
Page 93 © Lady Mairi Bury Estate.
Page 184 © Peter Clover.
Page 158 © Cobbe Collection.
Pages 27, 41 (left) © Country Life Picture Library.
Pages 188, 189 © Sir Edward Dashwood.
Page 55 © Getty Images/Gamma-Keystone; Page 116 © Getty Images/ Hulton Archive.
Pages 72, 140 © Petworth House Archives (Courtesy of Lord Egremont).
Pages 56, 57 © Rachel Hay.
Pages 92, 94 © Col. R. Meinertzhagen Estate.
Page 7 © William Henry Fox Talbot /National Media Museum / Science & Society Picture Library.
Pages 42 (below), 54 © National Trust/ Special Collections, University of Sussex .
Pages 15, 24, 163 © West Suffolk Record Office.
Page 73 (right) © Kevis Collection, West Sussex Record Office.

Index of Houses